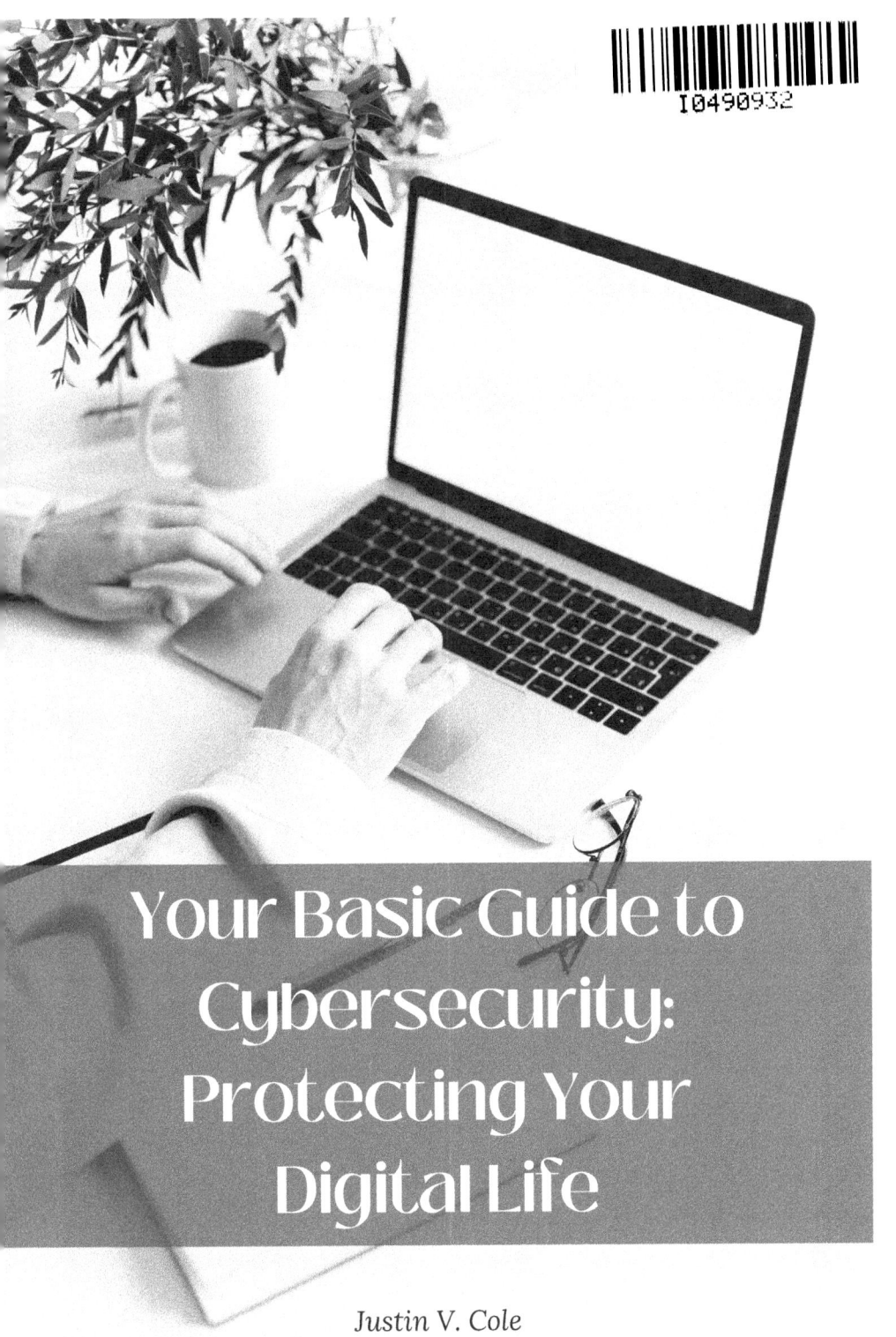

Your Basic Guide to Cybersecurity: Protecting Your Digital Life

Justin V. Cole

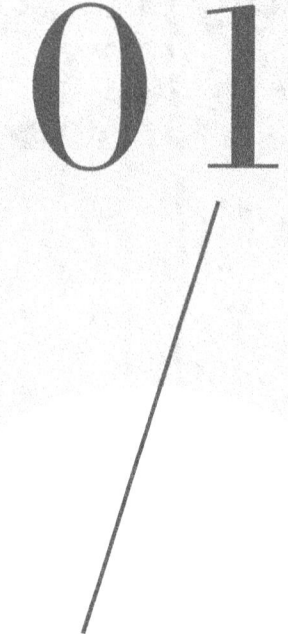

C H A P T E R

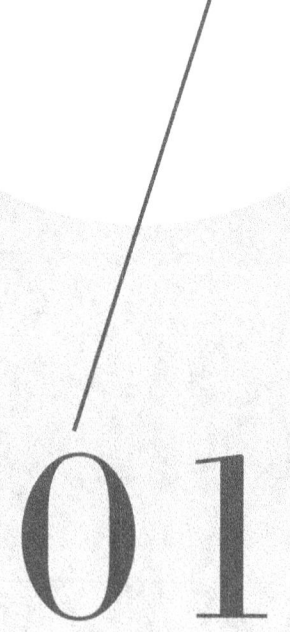

Chapter 1: Introduction to Cybersecurity and the C-I-A Triad

As technology has become essential to our lives, we must protect our digital assets from cyber threats. Cybersecurity protects electronic devices, networks, and sensitive information from cyber threats. Cyber threats are any attempt to steal, damage, or exploit personal or sensitive information through technology. The C-I-A triad (Confidentiality, Integrity, and Accessibility) is a framework used in cybersecurity that emphasizes the three essential components of secure information systems.

Confidentiality refers to keeping sensitive information private and secure from unauthorized access. In cybersecurity, sensitive information may include personal identifying information, intellectual property, financial data, and other sensitive information that could be exploited by cyber attackers.

Integrity refers to the accuracy and reliability of information. Maintaining integrity is essential because cyber attackers may modify, delete or destroy sensitive information to harm individuals or organizations. In cybersecurity, maintaining the integrity of sensitive information is vital to prevent unauthorized access, manipulation, or loss.

Accessibility refers to ensuring that authorized users have access to the resources they need to do their job effectively while keeping unauthorized users out. In cybersecurity, accessibility is vital to prevent cyber attackers from accessing sensitive information, such as login credentials, network resources, and sensitive data.

Cybersecurity threats come in various forms, including viruses, malware, phishing attacks, social engineering, and more. Cyber attackers can use these threats to gain unauthorized access to sensitive information, damage data, or even take control of entire systems.

Protecting the C-I-A Triad

The C-I-A triad is essential for maintaining the security of electronic devices, networks, and sensitive information. To ensure that the C-I-A triad is protected, it is necessary to use cybersecurity best practices. Here are a few key best practices:

Confidentiality:

- Use encryption to protect sensitive information: When sending sensitive information, use encrypted email services or messaging apps to ensure that the information is protected and cannot be intercepted by cyber attackers.
- Implement access controls to ensure that only authorized users can access sensitive information: Use strong passwords and never share them with anyone. Also, avoid using public Wi-Fi networks for sensitive transactions, as they may not be secure.
- Train employees or family members on handling sensitive information: Educate them on the importance of not sharing sensitive information with anyone

- unauthorized to access it and how to recognize and avoid phishing emails.

Integrity:
- Use backup and recovery systems to ensure that data is not lost or compromised: Regularly back up your important data to a secure location, such as an external hard drive or cloud storage. This ensures that your important data will be recovered if your device is lost, stolen, or damaged.
- Implement access controls to prevent unauthorized modifications or deletions of sensitive data: Use access controls to ensure that only authorized users can modify or delete sensitive information.
- Use data validation techniques to ensure that data is accurate and reliable: Double-check it for accuracy and completeness before entering data into a system.

Accessibility:
- Implement access controls to ensure that only authorized users can access sensitive information and network resources: Access controls can be implemented in various

- including using usernames and passwords, two-factor authentication, biometric authentication, and other methods. The specific method used will depend on the protected system or resource and the required security level.
- Use strong passwords and two-factor authentication to ensure only authorized users can access sensitive information and network resources. Also, avoid using the same password for multiple accounts.
- Keep software and operating systems up to date to prevent vulnerabilities that could be exploited by cyber attackers: Regularly update your software and operating systems to ensure that you have the latest security patches installed. This helps prevent cyber attackers from exploiting known vulnerabilities to gain unauthorized access to your device or sensitive information.

Conclusion

In this chapter, we introduced the concept of cybersecurity and the C-I-A triad. We also discussed how cyber threats can harm the confidentiality, integrity, and accessibility of sensitive information and the importance of protecting these three components. In the following chapters of this e-book, we will explore various cybersecurity topics in more detail, including best practices for online safety, securing your devices, protecting your network, and more, all with the central theme of maintaining the C-I-A triad. By implementing best practices and understanding the C-I-A triad, you can help protect yourself and your sensitive information from cyber

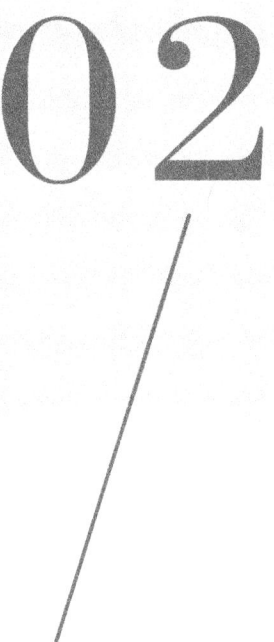

C H A P T E R

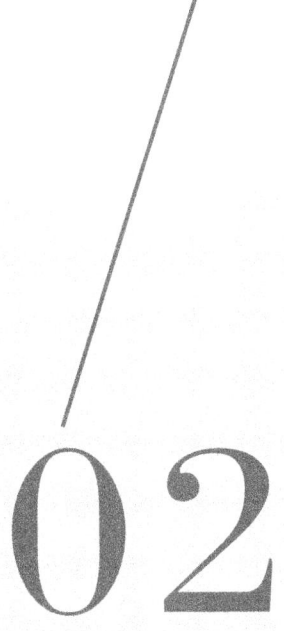

Chapter 2: Types of Cyber Threats

In today's digital age, cyber threats pose a significant risk to individuals and organizations. Cyber threats are any attempt to steal, damage, or exploit personal or sensitive information through technology. This chapter will define different types of cyber threats and explain how they can harm individuals and organizations.

Viruses
A virus is a type of malware that can replicate itself and spread from one device to another. Once a virus infects a device, it can cause many problems, such as slowing down the device, deleting files, and stealing personal information. Viruses can be spread through email attachments, infected software, and malicious websites. For example, the infamous "ILOVEYOU" virus in 2000 caused widespread damage by infecting millions of computers through email attachments.

Malware

Malware is a term used to describe any software designed to harm a device or steal personal information. Malware can come in many forms, including viruses, spyware, and ransomware. Spyware is a type of malware that can monitor a user's activity on a device and steal personal information. At the same time, ransomware is a type of malware that can lock a user out of their device and demand payment to regain access. Malware can be spread through email attachments, infected software, and malicious websites.

Phishing

Phishing is a type of cyber-attack that involves tricking a user into providing personal information, such as login credentials or credit card information. Phishing attacks can take many forms, such as fake emails, fake websites, or phone calls from counterfeit representatives of a legitimate organization. Phishing attacks can be used to steal personal information or spread malware.

For example, a phishing email that appears to be from a legitimate bank might ask the user to enter their login credentials, which can then be used to steal their personal information.

Social Engineering
Social engineering is a method cyber attackers use to manipulate individuals into divulging sensitive information or performing actions that benefit the attacker. Social engineering attacks can take many forms, such as phishing emails, phone calls from fake representatives of a legitimate organization, or even physical access to a device or network. Social engineering attacks can steal personal information, spread malware, or gain unauthorized access to a device or network.

Conclusion

This chapter defined different types of cyber threats and explained how they can harm individuals and organizations. We provided examples of each threat, including viruses, malware, phishing, and social engineering. By understanding the different types of cyber threats, individuals and organizations can take steps to protect themselves from these threats. In the following chapters of this e-book, we will discuss best practices for protecting devices, networks, and sensitive information from cyber threats.

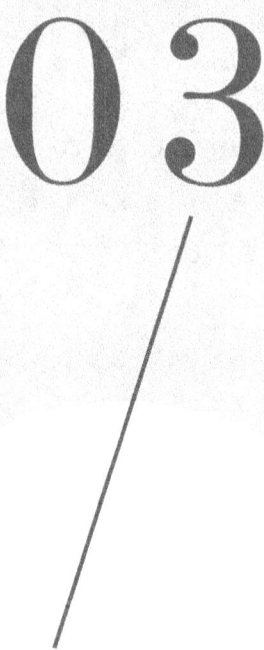

C H A P T E R

Chapter 3: How Cyber-Attacks Work

Cyber-attacks are attempts by cybercriminals to gain unauthorized access to personal or sensitive information. Cyber-attacks can take many forms, including social engineering, brute-force attacks, and malware. In this chapter, we will explain how cyber attackers gain access to personal and sensitive information, describe the methods used by cyber attackers, and provide examples of cyber-attacks and how they affect the C-I-A triad.

How Cyber Attackers Gain Access
Cyber attackers can gain access to personal and sensitive information in many ways. Some common methods include:

- Social Engineering: Social engineering is a method used by cyber attackers to manipulate individuals into divulging sensitive information or performing actions that benefit the attacker. Social engineering attacks can take many forms, such as

- phishing emails or phone calls from fake representatives of a legitimate organization. A social engineering attack affects the Confidentiality aspect of the C-I-A triad.
- Brute-Force Attacks: A brute-force attack is a method used by cyber attackers to gain access to a system or account by trying every possible combination of usernames and passwords until the correct one is found. A brute-force attack affects the Accessibility aspect of the C-I-A triad.
- Exploiting Vulnerabilities: Cyber attackers can exploit vulnerabilities in software or hardware to gain unauthorized access to a device or network. These vulnerabilities can be found through extensive research, or they may be publicly known and not yet patched. An attack exploiting vulnerabilities can affect all three aspects of the C-I-A triad.

Methods Used by Cyber Attackers

Once cyber attackers gain access to a device or network, they may use various methods to attack. Some common techniques used by cyber attackers include:

- Malware: Malware is software designed to harm a device or steal personal information. Cyber attackers may use malware to access sensitive information, spread it to other devices or networks, or lock users out of their devices or networks. A malware attack can affect the Confidentiality, Integrity, and Accessibility aspects of the C-I-A triad.

- Ransomware: Ransomware is malware that locks users out of their devices or networks and demands payment to regain access. Cyber attackers may use ransomware to extort money from individuals or organizations. A ransomware attack affects the Accessibility aspect of the C-I-A triad.

- DDoS Attacks: A DDoS (Distributed Denial of Service) attack is used by cyber attackers to overwhelm a network or

- server with traffic, causing it to crash or become unavailable. Cyber attackers may use DDoS attacks to disrupt organizations' operations or distract IT personnel from other attacks. A DDoS attack affects the Accessibility aspect of the C-I-A triad.

Examples of Cyber Attacks
Here are some examples of cyber attacks that have occurred in recent years:
- Equifax Breach: In 2017, Equifax, a credit reporting agency, suffered a data breach that exposed the personal information of millions of people. The breach was caused by an unpatched vulnerability in the software used by Equifax. An attack exploiting vulnerabilities can affect all three aspects of the C-I-A triad.
- WannaCry Ransomware: In 2017, the WannaCry ransomware spread to over 200,000 devices in 150 countries. The ransomware encrypted files on infected devices and demanded payment for a decryption key. A ransomware attack affects the accessibility aspect of the C-I-A triad.

- Target Breach: In 2013, Target suffered a data breach that exposed the personal information of more than 40 million customers. The breach was caused by a cyber attacker gaining access to Target's network through a third-party vendor. An attack exploiting vulnerabilities can affect all three aspects of the C-I-A triad.

Conclusion

In this chapter, we explained how cyber attackers gain access to personal and sensitive information, described the methods used by cyber attackers, and provided examples of cyber-attacks and how they affect the C-I-A triad. By understanding how cyber-attacks work and how they affect the C-I-A triad, individuals and organizations can take steps to protect themselves from these threats. In the following chapters of this e-book, we will discuss best practices for protecting devices, networks, and sensitive information from cyber-attacks.

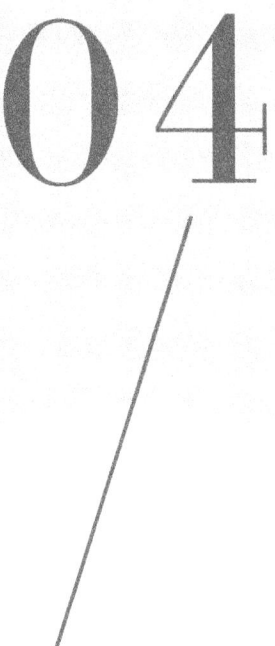

CHAPTER

Chapter 4: Protecting Your Digital Identity

Protecting your digital identity is more important than ever in the digital age. Your digital identity includes all the personal and sensitive information you have stored on your devices or online, such as your name, address, social security number, and financial information. In this chapter, we will explain the importance of protecting your digital identity, provide tips for creating strong passwords, explain the concept of two-factor authentication, and describe how to protect yourself from phishing attacks.

Importance of Protecting Your Digital Identity Protecting your digital identity is essential to maintaining the confidentiality, integrity, and accessibility of your personal and sensitive information. Hackers and cyber attackers constantly seek ways to access and exploit personal information, such as through social engineering or malware attacks. By protecting your digital identity, you can help prevent unauthorized access to your information, maintain its accuracy and completeness and ensure you have access to it when needed.

Creating Strong Passwords
Creating strong passwords is critical in protecting your digital identity (Confidentiality). A strong password is complicated for cyber attackers to guess or crack and is at least 12 characters long. Some tips for creating strong passwords include:

- Avoid using obvious words or phrases like "password" or "123456."
- Use uppercase and lowercase letters, numbers, and special characters.
- Avoid using the same password for multiple accounts.
- Use a "passphrase" that is easy to remember but hard for someone else to guess. Instead of using a simple word like "password," you could create a passphrase that is easy for you to remember but difficult for others to guess. For example, you could use the phrase "I love spending time at the beach with my family" and turn it into a strong password

using the first letter of each word, along with some numbers and special characters. Your resulting password could be: "Ilst@tBwmf!O1". This password is long, complex, and includes a mix of uppercase and lowercase letters, numbers, and special characters, making it difficult for cyber attackers to guess or crack.

Using Two-Factor Authentication

Two-factor authentication is an extra layer of security that requires you to provide two different forms of identification before accessing an account or device (Confidentiality and Integrity). This can include a password and a verification code sent to your phone or a fingerprint scan and a password. Two-factor authentication can help prevent unauthorized access to your accounts and devices. It can add an additional layer of protection to your digital identity.

Protecting Yourself from Phishing Attacks
Phishing attacks are a common method cyber attackers use to trick individuals into providing personal or sensitive information (Confidentiality). Phishing attacks can take many forms, such as fake emails, fake websites, or phone calls from fake representatives of a legitimate organization. To protect yourself from phishing attacks, you should:

- Be wary of emails or messages from unknown or suspicious senders.
- Avoid clicking on links or downloading attachments from unknown or suspicious sources.
- Verify the authenticity of personal or sensitive information requests by contacting the organization directly.

Conclusion

In this chapter, we explained the importance of protecting your digital identity. We provided tips for creating strong passwords, using two-factor authentication, and protecting yourself from phishing attacks. By following these best practices, you can help protect the confidentiality, integrity, and accessibility of your personal and sensitive information. In the following chapters of this e-book, we will discuss additional best practices for protecting devices, networks, and sensitive information from cyber-attacks.

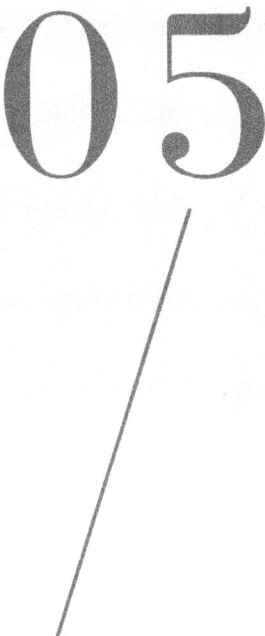

CHAPTER

Chapter 5: Secure Online Practices

The internet has become an integral part of our daily lives. Still, it also presents various risks to our digital security. Cyber attackers can use the internet to steal personal information, infect devices with malware, and carry out other attacks. This chapter will provide best practices for using the internet safely, explain how to identify and avoid scams, describe the importance of keeping software and operating systems up to date, and determine which portion of the C-I-A triad each best practice is supporting.

Using the Internet Safely
Using the internet safely is essential to maintaining the confidentiality, integrity, and accessibility of your personal and sensitive information. Some best practices for using the internet safely include:

- Avoid clicking on suspicious links or visiting suspicious websites (Confidentiality).
- Use a trusted antivirus program to protect your device from malware and other threats (Integrity).
- Enable your device's firewall to block unauthorized access to your device (Confidentiality).
- Use a VPN (Virtual Private Network) when accessing the internet from public Wi-Fi networks (Confidentiality).

Identifying and Avoiding Scams
Scammers use various tactics to trick individuals into providing personal or sensitive information, such as fake emails, fake websites, or phone calls from fake representatives of legitimate organizations. To identify and avoid scams, you should:

- Be wary of emails or messages from unknown or suspicious senders (Confidentiality).
- Avoid clicking links or downloading attachments from unknown or suspicious sources (Integrity).
- Verify the authenticity of requests for personal or sensitive information by contacting the organization directly (Confidentiality).

Keeping Software and Operating Systems Up to Date

Keeping your software and operating systems up to date is essential in maintaining the confidentiality, integrity, and accessibility of your personal and sensitive information. Software and operating system updates often include security patches that address vulnerabilities and other security issues.

Some best practices for keeping software and operating systems up to date include:

- Enable automatic updates for your software and operating systems (Integrity).
- Download updates only from trusted sources (Integrity).
- Use the latest version of your software and operating systems whenever possible (Integrity).

Conclusion

In this chapter, we provided best practices for using the internet safely, explained how to identify and avoid scams, and described the importance of keeping software and operating systems up to date. By following these best practices, you can help protect the confidentiality, integrity, and accessibility of your personal and sensitive information. In the following chapters of this e-book, we will discuss additional best practices for protecting devices, networks, and sensitive information from cyber-attacks and how they relate to the C-I-A triad.

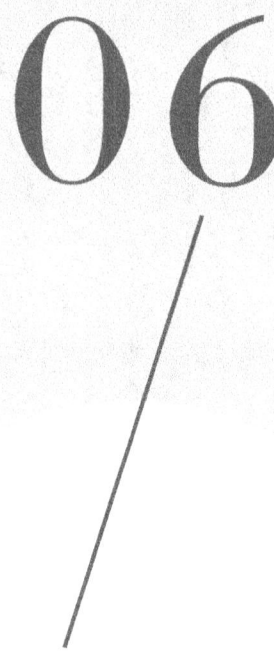

C H A P T E R

Chapter 6: Protecting Your Devices

In today's digital age, our devices are more vulnerable than ever to cyber threats. Cyber attackers can use various methods to access our devices and steal personal and sensitive information. This chapter will describe how to secure your devices from cyber threats, explain how to use antivirus software, and provide tips for protecting your mobile devices.

Securing Your Devices from Cyber Threats
Securing your devices from cyber threats is essential in protecting the confidentiality, integrity, and accessibility of your personal and sensitive information. Some best practices for securing your devices from cyber threats include:

- Use strong and unique passwords for each device (Confidentiality).
- Use two-factor authentication to add an additional layer of protection (Integrity).
- Enable automatic updates for your operating system and applications (Integrity).

- Use a firewall to block unauthorized access to your device (Confidentiality).
- Use a VPN (Virtual Private Network) when accessing the internet from public Wi-Fi networks (Confidentiality).
- Disable unused services and features on your device to reduce the attack surface (Integrity).

Using Antivirus Software

Antivirus software is critical in protecting your device from malware and other cyber threats. Antivirus software can scan your device for viruses and other malware and prevent them from infecting it. Some best practices for using antivirus software include:

- Use reputable and up-to-date antivirus software (Integrity).
- Enable automatic updates for your antivirus software (Integrity).
- Perform regular scans of your device (Integrity).

Protecting Your Mobile Devices

Mobile devices like smartphones and tablets are also vulnerable to cyber threats. Some best practices for protecting your mobile devices include:

- Use a passcode or biometric authentication to secure your device (Confidentiality).
- Enable automatic updates for your operating system and applications (Integrity).
- Be cautious when downloading and installing apps from unknown or untrusted sources (Integrity).
- Use a VPN (Virtual Private Network) when accessing the internet from public Wi-Fi networks (Confidentiality).
- Avoid clicking suspicious links or downloading attachments from unknown or questionable sources (Integrity).

Conclusion

In this chapter, we described how to secure your devices from cyber threats, how to use antivirus software, and provided tips for protecting your mobile devices. By following these best practices, you can help protect the confidentiality, integrity, and accessibility of your personal and sensitive information. In the following chapters of this e-book, we will discuss additional best practices for protecting networks and sensitive information from cyber-attacks while continuing to tie the concepts and examples to the C-I-A triad.

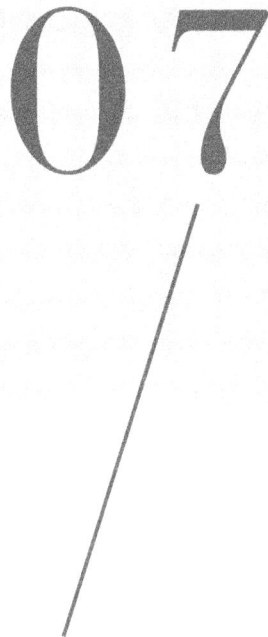

07

CHAPTER

07

Chapter 7: Protecting Your Network

In addition to securing your devices, your home or office network is vital. Cyber attackers can use unsecured networks to access your devices and steal personal and sensitive information. This chapter will explain the importance of securing your home or office network, provide tips for securing your Wi-Fi network, and explain how to create a secure network password.

Securing Your Wi-Fi Network
Securing your Wi-Fi network is essential in protecting the confidentiality, integrity, and accessibility of your personal and sensitive information. Some best practices for securing your Wi-Fi network include:
- Change the default name and password of your Wi-Fi network (Integrity).
- Enable WPA2 (Wi-Fi Protected Access II) encryption on your Wi-Fi network (Confidentiality).

- Use a strong and unique password for your Wi-Fi network (Integrity).
- Disable or limit guest access to a separate guest network (Confidentiality).
- Disable remote management of your router (Integrity).

Creating a Secure Network Password
Creating a secure network password is essential in protecting the confidentiality, integrity, and accessibility of your home or office network. The best practices for creating a secure network password include mirroring those for creating a secure personal password:

- Use a long and complex password that is difficult to guess (Integrity).
- Use a mix of uppercase and lowercase letters, numbers, and special characters in your password (Integrity).
- Avoid using common or easily guessable words or phrases (Integrity).
- Avoid using personal information, such as your name or birthdate, in your password (Confidentiality).

Conclusion

In this chapter, we explained the importance of securing your home or office network, provided tips for securing your Wi-Fi network, and explained how to create a secure network password. By following these best practices, you can help protect the confidentiality, integrity, and accessibility of your personal and sensitive information. In the following and final chapter of this e-book, we will summarize the key takeaways from this book and provide additional resources for further learning about cybersecurity.

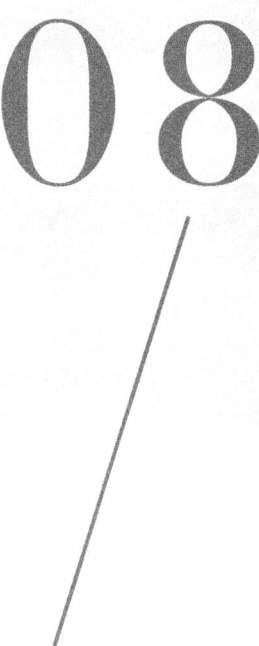

CHAPTER

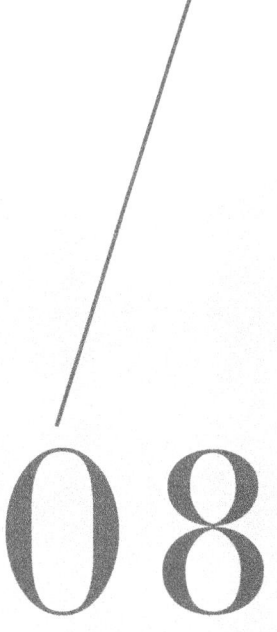

Chapter 8: Cybersecurity Resources

Learning about cybersecurity is an ongoing process. Many resources are available to help you stay current on the latest best practices and trends. This chapter will provide a list of cybersecurity resources for further learning, including links to government cybersecurity agencies, industry associations, and cybersecurity experts.

Government Cybersecurity Agencies
Government cybersecurity agencies provide valuable resources and information on cybersecurity best practices and threats. Some examples of government cybersecurity agencies include:

- United States Computer Emergency Readiness Team (US-CERT) - https://www.us-cert.gov/
- National Cyber Security Centre (NCSC) - https://www.ncsc.gov.uk/

Australian Cyber Security Centre (ACSC) - https://www.cyber.gov.au/

- Cybersecurity and Infrastructure Security Agency (CISA) - https://www.cisa.gov/cybersecurity

CISA is the US government's lead agency for protecting the country's critical infrastructure from cyber threats. The agency provides resources and services to organizations and individuals to help them protect their networks and systems from cyber-attacks. Their website offers a wealth of information on cybersecurity best practices, including tips on securing networks, protecting against malware and ransomware, and responding to cyber incidents.

Industry Associations
Industry associations provide valuable resources and networking opportunities for cybersecurity professionals. Some examples of industry associations include:
- Information Systems Security Association (ISSA) - https://www.issa.org/
- Cloud Security Alliance (CSA) - https://cloudsecurityalliance.org/

- International Association of Computer Science and Information Technology (IACSIT) - https://www.iacsit.org/

Cybersecurity Experts
Cybersecurity experts provide valuable insights and expertise on cybersecurity trends and threats. Some examples of cybersecurity experts include:
- Bruce Schneier - https://www.schneier.com/
- Mikko Hyppönen - https://mikkohypponen.com/
- Brian Krebs - https://krebsonsecurity.com/

Conclusion

This chapter provided a list of cybersecurity resources for further learning, including links to government cybersecurity agencies, industry associations, and cybersecurity experts. By utilizing these resources, you can stay informed and educated about the latest cybersecurity best practices and threats and help protect the confidentiality, integrity, and accessibility of your personal and sensitive information.

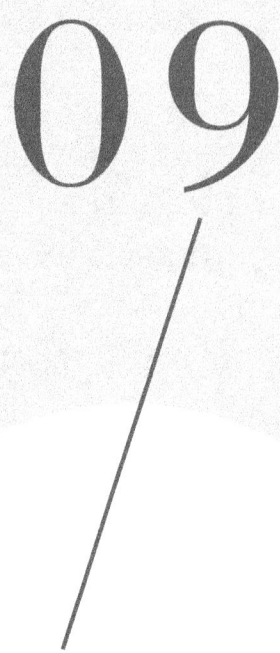

C H A P T E R

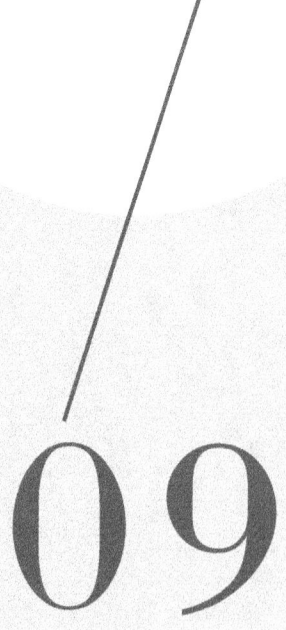

Chapter 9: Conclusion

Congratulations! You've reached the end of our e-book on cybersecurity basics. In this final chapter, we will summarize the key takeaways from this book and encourage you to take action to improve your cybersecurity.

Key Takeaways
Throughout this e-book, we've covered a lot of ground on the basics of cybersecurity. Here are the key takeaways:

- Confidentiality, integrity, and accessibility are the three components of the C-I-A triad essential to protecting your personal and sensitive information from cyber threats.
- Cyber threats come in many forms, including viruses, malware, phishing, and social engineering attacks. By understanding these threats, you can better protect yourself against them.

- Protecting your digital identity is crucial in today's digital age. Creating strong passwords, using two-factor authentication, and avoiding phishing attacks are essential to safeguard your personal and sensitive information.
- Safe online practices, such as avoiding suspicious links and websites, identifying and avoiding scams, and keeping software and operating systems up to date, can help protect your personal and sensitive information.
- Protecting your devices and networks from cyber threats is essential to safeguarding your personal and sensitive information. Using antivirus software, protecting your mobile devices, securing your Wi-Fi network, and creating a secure network password are essential steps to take.

Take Action
Now that you've learned about the basics of cybersecurity, it's time to take action to improve your cybersecurity posture. Here are some steps you can take:

- Regularly update your passwords and use two-factor authentication whenever possible to protect your digital identity.
- Avoid clicking suspicious links or opening attachments from unknown senders to protect against phishing attacks.
- Keep your software and operating systems up to date to ensure that security patches are installed promptly.
- Use antivirus software to protect your devices from malware and other cyber threats.
- Secure your Wi-Fi network by changing the default name and password, enabling WPA2 encryption, using a strong and unique password, disabling guest access, and disabling remote management.

By taking these steps, you can help protect the confidentiality, integrity, and accessibility of your personal and sensitive information.

Conclusion

In conclusion, this e-book has provided you with a solid foundation in cybersecurity basics. Remember, cybersecurity is an ongoing process, and staying informed and educated is essential to protecting your personal and sensitive information. By following the best practices outlined in this e-book and utilizing the resources provided, you can help protect yourself from cyber threats and safeguard your personal and sensitive information. Thank you for reading!